John Clark Ridpath

The Citizen Soldier

John Clark Ridpath

The Citizen Soldier

ISBN/EAN: 9783337308124

Printed in Europe, USA, Canada, Australia, Japan

Cover: Foto ©ninafisch / pixelio.de

More available books at **www.hansebooks.com**

THE

CITIZEN SOLDIER.

THE CITIZEN SOLDIER

HIS PART IN WAR AND PEACE.

. . . . .

· BY ·

JOHN CLARK RIDPATH

. . . . .

"THEIR RISING ALL AT ONCE WAS AS THE SOUND
OF THUNDER HEARD REMOTE."
                                        —MILTON.

· 1892 ·

THE MEN WHO MADE THE NATION FREE—
WHO BORE THE FLAG OF GLORY
THROUGH BATTLE-BLAST TO VICTORY—
THE UNCROWNED KINGS OF STORY.

THE CITIZEN SOLDIER.

LADIES AND GENTLEMEN:

Amid the commemorative services of this day we may well pause to consider the character and deeds of the Citizen Soldier. In the history of the world the soldier has performed the largest part. From the primitive ages until the present day he has been the most powerful single factor among the forces which have contributed to the civilization of mankind. We have to reflect, in this connection, that the history of civilization has been the history of violence. The present refinement and progress of the human race did not begin in peaceful and beautiful gardens; in happy spots by the river banks; in flower-decked islands where golden apples grow; but in cruel savagery and the bloody jungles of barbarism.

Out of such a condition it was impossible for man to emerge except by force. In his rudest estate he had to make his way by sword and spear and battle-axe. Every pathway which he trod had to be hewed, not only through the primitive thickets of the ancient

wilderness, but through the fiercest opposition of his
fellowmen. It must be remembered that in the primeval ages men subsisted on the gifts of the earth.
They gathered from the trees and water-brooks the
means of sustaining life. Here was the foundation
of that dreadful system of competition which to the
present day holds the world in its cruel grip. It may
be that in process of time this system of competition, which has wrought so great havoc with the peace
and happiness of mankind, will give place to the more
generous method of coöperation, under the reign of
which our fellow beings shall work shoulder to shoulder, instead of striving, as they have always done,
face to face.

This is the genesis of the soldier. He appeared in
the world as an agent for correcting violence with
other violence more humane. The world was given
up to force, not to say brutality, and the soldier came
to make the reign of force more tolerable, the brutality less brutal. In order to understand his relation
to the history of the world we must consider that
history as a long series of slow and toilsome advances
from the darkness and violence of the beginning to
the comparative light and reason of a happier age.
In this respect the world has been grievously mis-
taken. Men have fondly flattered themselves with

the dream of a primitive Golden Age in which the
ancestors of the race were somewhat as the angels,
walking and communing with their fellows; loving
each the other as himself; ministering to the misfor-
tunes of the few; aspiring to be as the gods. It is
only a dream—a phantasm of the poet's imagination—
with no similitude in fact. We now know that the
beginnings of human progress were with the wild
creatures of the primeval woods, and in the dripping
caves where extinct bears and hyenas had their lair.

How hardly did man come forth from such a state
and begin his career of progress and amelioration!
How hardly did he rise to the integrity of thought and
the purity of conscience. We may well understand
how toilsome and tedious has been the human march.
The rise of man has been as slow as the process of the
suns. History has had to invent a calculus in order to
discover the almost imperceptible movement of mankind toward the light. Thousands upon thousands of
years have passed away while this tedious history has
been enacting, and even yet the emergence of man is
far from perfect. He lingers still, like Milton's lion,
with his hinder parts in the hillsides of barbarism.
Only his better parts have been eliminated from the
original dirt, out of which, by some process, he was
taken.

The soldier of antiquity was indeed a man of
blood. We are constrained to say that he was a
homicide by profession. He was the easy chief of all
butchery. It was his business not only to kill, but to
exterminate. The discipline of his murderous voca-
tion made him at once a cunning and ferocious
destroyer of life. Several circumstances conspired to
make him conspicuous above all other destructive
agents as the prime hunter and killer of the world.
In the first place, his own barbarous and almost con-
scienceless character conduced to the freedom which
he felt and rejoiced in as a slayer of men. It is difficult for us in this age to conceive the sentiments, and
emotions, and passions of the ancient warrior. In
order to do so we have to feel our way backward by
imagination through centuries of time and continents
of space. Even when we have reached the station of
the old time man of battle and slaughter, we are
unable to enter into his feelings; share his impulses;
or think his thoughts. The picturesque Taine has
told us that of all hunts the man-hunt is the most
noble and glorious. Doubtless it was so according to
the standard of antiquity. We read of the horrid
butcheries which have preserved to themselves a
name and memory in the pages of ancient history.
We draw back in horror from the picture of one of

those ancient battle-fields heaped with its dead and
dying, red with an ocean of blood pouring from the
gashes in forty thousand breasts; but we fail to
remember that the other aspects of the life of
antiquity were equally ferocious and dreadful.

It was not, however, the innate savage nature only
of the ancient battle-man that made him what he was.
The theory of warfare which prevailed among all the
ancient nations conduced to the same end. Nothing
indeed can be more unlike another thing, belonging to
the same class of facts with itself, than was ancient
warfare unlike the warfare of to-day. The motives
and principles governing the conduct of war in antiquity were sufficiently shocking and vicious. As a
rule, mere robbery was the inspiring cause of battle.
The men of one tribe seized upon the cattle of the
men of another tribe; drove them away; hid them in
caves and mountain gorges, and then took arms to
beat back the assailants who came in hot pursuit.
The tribesmen were much more concerned about the
protection of property than they were for the protection of life. One of seven brothers might be carried
away and sold into slavery without great offense to
the remaining six; but woe to the robbers who drove
away the flock or herd.

War once undertaken was a matter of personal

conflict. It was not only personal, but universal.
Every man of the one tribe was the sworn enemy of
every man of the other tribe. The law of war was
that each should take or kill his enemy on sight. He
might do it as he would, fairly or perfidiously, in
manly fight of the open field or by stealthy thrust of
the treacherous, and possibly the poisoned, spear in
the dark. Quarter there was none. Flag of truce
and armistice were as yet unknown. Division
between soldiery and citizenship, between the com-
batant and the non-combatant, had not yet been
drawn. The home and the product of the garden
and field were as little sacred as were the spears and
bows and slings of the enemy. All ages and sexes
and conditions were swept into the vortex. All
suffered alike at the hand of the invaders. The
woman and her child were a part of that common
enemy which the soldier of antiquity was pledged
to kill or enslave. The old man with white locks,
blossoming like the almond tree, and the rosy-cheeked
boy with his child eyes and lisping tongue were alike
thrust through and hurled down to death and oblivion.
Thought can not conceive, or tongue express, or
pen record the awful devastation, the woe, the
carnage, the fire, the blood, the death, and universal
wasting of that ancient savage warfare which was

undertaken, not for the lawful redress of grievances or the maintenance of human rights, but under the vindictiveness of sheer passion and the blind rage of personal wrong.

As the chaotic society of the primitive ages was slowly evolved into higher conditions of life, the soldier was separated from the other social forces and became a distinct energy. He was dissociated from his fellows who, on the one hand, tilled the soil, and, on the other, ruled the State. He stood on the plane of the priesthood. Upon these two, the soldier and the priest, the king leaned as the principal pillars of support to his dynasty and throne.

The condition as a whole is easily apprehended. The institution of monarchy universally prevailed. It can not be doubted that the monarchical form of government is natural and inevitable in certain stages of human society. It is equally certain that a professional priesthood and a professional soldiery are the necessary concomitants of monarchy. A king does not rule by right, reason, or the rational consent of his subjects. He is arrogant enough to say that his right to rule is the gift of Heaven, and that so far as earthly relations are concerned, his place at the head of society is determined by the accident of birth.

It were hard to say which of these two assumptions

is the more absurd. He who is fool enough to say that his civil authority is derived from on high instead of given by his fellowmen, may well be fool enough to claim a kingly rank in virtue of his birth. But whatever may be the genesis of the king, he has always found it necessary to buttress his throne with two things: force and superstition. The latter he has found abundantly supplied by the priests, and the former he has obtained in a professional soldiery.

The great monarchies of antiquity were monuments of superstition and force. Armies of hardy and hardened soldiers were organized and maintained at the expense of the State, and were used by the king in enforcing his will, not only in civil administration, but in foreign war. The ancient army was a sort of battering-ram in the hands of the king. He set it up before the walls of his rebellious city, and the walls crumbled. He planted it before the gates of his enemy's capital, and the pillars thereof were battered down. In either event, pillage and ruin, fire and death, followed the catastrophe. License in all its forms was the gift of victory.

What the individual warrior had been in the first ages of the world, that the army now became on a gigantic scale. The ancient army was a devouring monster, the breadth of whose bloody jaws, the depth

of whose ravenous throat, the rage of whose burning
lust, no pen could picture. Perhaps it was necessary
in the order of things that such a beast should be
loosed in the world. The student of history has at
length come to understand that under certain conditions physical evil is moral force, and that much must
be destroyed in order that a few things may live. He
has come to know that nature herself, such as she is
in a world like ours, is cruel, heartless, and blind, as
well as tender, compassionate, and loving. The
ancient army, horrible engine that it was, performed
its part in the history of civilization and has hardly
yet ceased to bray mankind in a mortar.

It was an interesting and happy phase in the
progress of the civilized life of man when the first
touches and pencilings of the nobler sentiments were
seen on the brow of war. Soldiers of all ranks and
conditions in all parts of the world may well be proud
of the fact that mediæval Europe felt the first glow of
moral enthusiasm in the ranks of her soldiery. It was
at the close of the crusading epoch. Hundreds and
thousands of European soldiers had joined their forces
and set their faces to the East. There, in the City of
David, the Infidel Turk sat cross-legged, smoking his
pipe, and whetting his blade on the tomb of Christ.
Most of the battlemen of the West perished in the

Holy Wars, but the rest came back with the seeds of chivalry in their breasts.

Ever afterwards there was seen, in greater brilliance or less, the new light of humanity on the soldier's helmet. True, the armies of Europe were destined for several centuries still to uphold and perpetuate the ferocious sentiments of antiquity and to practice the bloody butcheries of the past. But the dawn had come, and the day was sure to rise when the man of war should become as humane and honorable amid the carnage of the field and the storming of cities as the man of peace had already become in the tillage of his field and the shopwork of his hamlet.

The next striking phase in the evolution of the soldier was that which presents him under the garb of a citizen. There came to pass in the world, at length, a Citizen Soldier. The presence of such a fact among the energies of civilization implies several things. It implies, in the first place, the existence of some motive of warlike action sufficiently powerful to sway a multitude with a common passion. It signifies a popular recognition of some wrong that must be righted by force, some injustice that must be cured with the sword, some turpitude in human society that must be washed away with blood. Such motives of action can never appeal to a professional soldiery.

Warriors who are hired and disciplined in the art of destruction, as one may be taught architecture or dancing, become a machine as incapable of conscience and sentiment as a catapult or a locomotive. But the citizen is a patriot. He loves his home, his kindred, his native land; and when occasion requires he draws the sword in their defense.

The beginnings of a citizen soldiery were seen in the Classical Ages of antiquity. The citizens of Greece rose in times of the Persian invasion and dealt upon the foe the vengeance which only roused-up patriots are able to inflict. What the citizen converted into the soldier for the sake of native land is able to do by his valor was demonstrated for all ages at Marathon, at Platæa, at Salamis. In primitive Rome something of the same thing was seen. The sturdy patriots of the Republic left their plows in the field at the call of the Senate, and interposed their rough breasts and brawny arms between the city and barbarous invasion.

But these were the exceptions to the general rule. The Roman armies in the times of the Empire were simply an aggregation of brute force wielded by terrified despots or ambitious demagogues.

In modern times we have seen the fuller and more glorious emergence of a citizen soldiery. So far as my study has extended, I should say that the first example of such a soldiery, on a grand scale, was furnished by the English armies in the times of the Commonwealth. Cromwell's Ironsides, psalm-singing bigots as they were, were, at the bottom, citizens who knew what they were fighting for, as well as they knew how to fight. On the other side the Cavaliers stood for the past. They stood for mediæval traditions as well as for mediæval government. They stood for aristocracy, for the divine right of kings, for the few against the many, and for the king against the few. They stood for ecclesiasticism, for arbitrary rule, license for those who have the power, and slavery for those who have it not. But the Cromwellian soldiery stood for the Under Man. It was a power that rose as if from the earth. It was of titanic grandeur. Its might was the might of a thunderbolt; its energies were the combined energies of that long repressed people who at length burst through the crust of tyranny and smote the tyrant with a fatal blow.

It remained, however, for the last quarter of the eighteenth century to exhibit in its purest form a true citizen soldiery. The future, better than the present, will understand for how many things History is indebted to this New World which we call

America. Our fathers were pioneers, not only of the great republican experiment in government, but of many other things almost as salutary and glorious. Among these other things the principle of patriotic self-defense by means of the people themselves, risen against wrong, armed for the occasion and commanded, strangely enough, by their own neighbors, was one of the most conspicuous facts. Our fathers of the Old Thirteen Colonies had little acquaintance with a professional soldiery, and that little was unfavorable in the last degree. The occasional regiments of regulars and mercenaries who from time to time made their way to the American shores were not of a character or bearing to impress themselves with favor upon the hardy and virtuous men of the Colonies. The latter looked ever askance at this foreign soldiery, and wished it back in its own place beyond the sea.

The struggle of these two forces, namely, the self-defending, patriotic, Colonial militia, on the one side, and the professional, mercenary, foreign army on the other, was conspicuously and memorably illustrated in the campaign of Braddock. We all recall the story. Ever after the dreadful disaster in which that campaign ended, the native, Colonial, citizen soldier became more and more powerful—

more and more the reliance of his own colony first, and then of all the colonies as represented in the Continental Congress.

During the Revolutionary era, our fathers created the noblest military contingent which had yet been seen in the tides of time. The Continental army was born of the earth. It sprang from the ground in the hour of peril. At first it was an object of derision and scorn to the disciplined and pampered legions which were sent against us. Undoubtedly there was cause for ridicule and laughter. We must remember the character of the throng which gathered around Boston, in 1775, for the expulsion of the British. The battle of Bunker Hill had just been fought. The news of it flew on the wings of the wind. The men of New England sprang to arms and came flocking from all quarters. Each had his own accoutrements and uniform. The accoutrements were powder-horn, bullet-moulds and rifle. The uniform was a signal failure. It had no likeness to anything but itself. Each was of its own kind and pattern. What an impression the motley throng— each intent on the one great business of firing a well-aimed block of lead into a Red-coat hireling—must have made on the sedate Washington, as he rode out under the Cambridge elm to take the command in chief! But there was mettle in such a soldiery. Every heart had its altar and its fire. There was an incense of patriotism rising above that unique camp more odorous in the nostrils of Heaven than the smell of burning bullocks in the courtyard of Solomon's temple.

The spirit thus enkindled in the New World soon flamed high, and its light was seen across the Atlantic. It were difficult to say to what extent the great Revolution which now came on in France was born of an enthusiasm which had its first warmth on this side of the sea. In that sunny land, also, a great soldiery arose as if by magic. Liberty put his bugle to his lips and blew a blast which echoed far against

"—— castle walls
And snowy summits old in story."

Never was seen a more glorious exhibition of patriotic force than that displayed by the French people in their wild charge for emancipation and the rights of man. No Austrian battery, no army of Emigrant Nobles, not all the combined cohorts of Feudal Europe could withstand the impetuous onset of the terrible French democracy, roaring like an avalanche, as it fell with irresistible force upon the enemy. Such was the burning vehemence of that onset that the very landmarks of civilization, set up centuries before by the kings and princes of the Middle Ages, were swept into oblivion. Traditions perished; ancient customs died in a night; the whole form and fashion of French society were made anew in the storm of battle, and Liberty, with flaming eyes and cap of Phrygia on her majestic brow, held aloft a gleaming sword-blade in the light of the new morning which had risen for the human race.

At the close of the great Revolutionary era, this magnificent citizen soldiery which had fought the battle of freedom, first in America and then in France, lost at once its warlike character and melted away among the people from whom it had sprung. These phenomena were new in the history of the world. Man had not hitherto displayed his activities in such a manner. The soldier of the war period resumed his relations in society, and became the citizen again in the period of peace. The principle had been perfectly demonstrated that the people of a nation are able to rise at the nation's call and defend it from harm. More than this, it was shown beyond the possibility of doubt that the people thus insurgent are able to seize the governing powers and compel them to the great work of reform. No man could any longer doubt that the civil society of America and of a large part of Western Europe had been regenerated by the revolt of the people and their conversion into armies.

The subsidence of the citizen soldiery to its former place and functions in the nation left at least two great and salutary benefits to mankind. The first of these was the effect which the people's army produced upon the army of the State. Hitherto, as we have seen, the soldier's work had been, for the most part, a kind of professional and mercenary butchery, done in the service of the State and frequently against the aspirations and best interests of the people. It was the business of the old-time army to fight whatever opposed it until the opposition was broken; to march about in obedience to the command of generals who were themselves commanded by the king; to camp and decamp; to plunder or refrain from plundering at the dictation of the State.

It was precisely such a force as this that the people's army, the great citizen soldiery, had to contend with in the American and French Revolutions. Opposing armies on battle-fields shoot into each other's breasts many other things besides lead. The battery throws not only iron but thought. Your musket is a great dispenser of sentiment. In an intelligent age, fighting men discharge their opinions at each other as forcibly as they discharge their bullets. Every storm is an agent and mode of equilibrium. The thunder-clouds send into each other their positive and negative flashes of light and heat. So of contending armies. This is to say that the regular soldiery, such as it was at the close of the eighteenth century, received in the shock of battle the sentiments of the people. While the people were learning to fight, the professional soldier was, for the first time in his life, learning to think. He saw that the people's army was alive with thought. He also perceived that it was heated with a patriotic enthusiasm to which he had hitherto been a stranger. He began to FEEL. Hitherto he had felt nothing. Hitherto he had been a machine, doing his work under the touch and monition of the general's sword. Now he saw a great soldiery moved by another force, and he recognized the superiority of the motive over that by which he himself had been impelled to battle.

From this time forth the hard and brutal outlines in the face of professional war began to relax and soften. Then it was, indeed, that grim-visaged war did smooth his wrinkled front. Henceforth the regular army held a changed relation to the people. The soldier by profession began to sympathize with the citizen soldier and to acknowledge his higher calling. Since the Revolutionary epoch, it has become almost

impossible to compel a European army to fight the
people. One army will fight another army. The
forces of one state will cross the border and confront
the forces of another state in deadly conflict, as of
old. But let a great city be shaken by an insurrection of the people; let the ruler send out his orders
to his regulars to fire upon the insurgents and run
them down with bayonet charges in the streets,
and the orders are at once disobeyed. Soldiers by
profession, in every capital of Europe, are no longer
trusted to butcher their fellow-citizens when they
rise with banners in their hands and assail the battle-
ments of power in some righteous insurrection. This
great change in the manners and sentiments of the
professional soldiery of the world has been produced
by its contact with the citizen soldiery new risen
from the people.

In the next place, the citizen soldiery of the Age
of Revolution taught the kings of the world a signifi-
cant and memorable lesson. Hitherto the rulers of
mankind had fondly imagined themselves infallible.
The monarchs of Europe had their dread of one
another; each feared that his fellow king was
stronger than himself, and that he might rise against
him by battle or diplomacy, and make him his vassal.
But none of them feared their subjects. All looked

upon the people as the mere material which kings and generals and priests must have for the necessary practice of their arts. The attitude of your sovereign toward his subject was, in this respect, much like that of the big medicine man of modern times whose profession would be a nullity if he had no material on which to expend his science and consume his drugs!

This coming of the citizen soldier, this manifestation of his power as an agent of progress and righteousness, was the beginning of a new era in the civilized life of man. It was in some sense the premonition of the reign of the people. The thing done in the great revolutions in our own country and in France became the principal impulse of a reformation which has already expanded over half the world. There is not a nation in all Europe west of the Vistula which has not been to some extent regenerated by the influences shed forth by the citizen soldiery of the French republican armies. The same is true in a still greater degree of the influence diffused by our own Revolutionary soldiery of 1776. The people everywhere have become conscious, not only of their political, but of their military power. Governments of all forms and fashions have taken a wholesome dread of the physical force resident in the people. It is at once instructive and amusing to witness the changed tone and bearing of your king, your prince, your emperor, and sometimes your president, when the ominous murmur of a dissatisfied and rising people is heard in the distance. The manners of our rulers have been greatly improved within the present century, and it is not impossible that with the lapse of another hundred years they may attain the stature and title of gentlemen.

It was one of the peculiarities of the ancient world that its Force and its Thought drew in opposite directions. What men thought, looked to certain ends which were still ideal and apparently unattainable. Plato conceived a REPUBLIC, and wrote the outlines of its structure and methods in a beautiful treatise which the highest minds of the world still peruse with delight. But his Republic was a dream. Not even the author conceived the possibility of such a government as a practical fact among men. All the physical forces of ancient society ran to despotism. They tended to the production of great consolidated structures — civil, political, and religious — under which mankind were pressed and flattened against the earth. The enterprises of society were not directed by thought, but by sheer ebullitions of passion and caprice. The thinker, the artist, the poet, the orator, the historian, wrought in one direction, and the king, the warrior, the priest, the noble, and even the slave, wrought in another ; so that society was distraught and pulled asunder between them.

Under such a condition there could be no social unity. The government was one thing, and the people—at least so many of the people as had risen to thought and conscience—were another thing. The physical energy of society dashed hither and yon like a wild beast plunging in the arena. All they who had attained to ideality, to the higher forms of conscious-ness and hope, drew apart from the wind of violence ; secluded themselves in shady places by green banks of flowing streams ; gave way to reverie ; imagined the forms and features of things unseen, and dreamed of beautiful nymphs dwelling in the woods and waters. It was thus that the thought of the ancient world inhabited a body with wings, while the force of antiquity resided in a beast with fangs and terrible claws. While the one traversed the air and bathed in cloud and sunlight, the other wallowed in swamps and caves, or came forth only to crush the bones of innocence and peace.

The citizen soldier did one of his noblest works in harmonizing the thought and force of the world. After his appearance — after his first ascendency at the close of the eighteenth century — force became humane, and thought a practical energy. The divorce which had held for so many ages between the dreams and the deeds of mankind was abolished, and henceforth the sons of Adam began to imagine what they would have, and to have what they imagined. Henceforth it was possible to do an ideal thing and to think a reality. True, the alienation between the thinking and the doing has not yet wholly passed away; but, thanks to the citizen soldier, it is no longer necessary that a poet should cease to eat the food of men, or that a king should be a dreamless idiot.

The history of the present century has been the history of the development of those principles in civil society for which the citizen soldiery rose and fought a hundred years ago. The progress of the European and American nations has been commensurate with the incorporation of those principles in the practices of men. Of a certainty, society has not at all times gone forward with equal pace. It is true that not every epoch and every condition is equally favorable for the production of a citizen soldiery or for the display of its highest qualities. Nations have their heroic ages, after which there is likely to supervene an epoch of lethargy and reaction. Man himself obeys the same law. He sometimes has a season of high resolve and

tremendous display of virtue, and at other times he
has his era of indolence, apathy and stupid sleep.

Here in our America we have seen these principles
often and amply illustrated. It is my purpose in the
remainder of the present discussion to limit the inquiry
to the United States, and to speak of the part which
our citizen soldiery has borne in the development
and maintenance of our nationality. After our heroic
age, at the close of the eighteenth century, there
was a lull in our history of the kind to which we have
just referred. It is certain that the men of 1812 were
not the men of the Revolution. I would not by
any means disparage the American soldiers who contended with the Mother Country in our second war
for national independence. But it is only the truth
of history that the war of 1812 was commonplace,
unheroic, without rational motives in its beginning,
or logical results in its end. You have only to glance
at the Treaty of Ghent to note that not a single one of
the alleged principles for which the war was undertaken was so much as mentioned in the compact with
which it was concluded. The war was, therefore,
an absurdity ; and it is impossible that an absurdity
should ever evoke a great citizen soldiery. This is
to say that the citizen soldier as distinguished from
the battleman of the Middle Ages must, if he fight

well, know what he is fighting for. In our second war with Great Britain, some of our armies rose at times almost to the heroic level. Scott and Brown, just beyond the rapids of Niagara, where the rising spray of the incomparable Falls caught the flashes of the setting sun and held aloft a hundred rainbows over the chasm while the British were hurled back from the heights of Chippewa, were on the level where the fathers had stood in the days of '76. The sturdy and inflexible Jackson behind his bulwark of cotton bales, telling his men of Tennessee to withhold their terrible fire till the fated soldiers of Pakenham were ready to leap the trenches, and then hurling them with one blast to defeat, destruction, and death, may be numbered with the men of the Revolution—with Sumter and Greene and Putnam and Mad Anthony Wayne.

For the rest, the war of 1812 was tame and weak —vague in its methods, feeble in its execution. We had had an outcry about "Free Trade and Sailors' Rights"; but the Free Trade was a more uncertain thing than it has since become on the lips of American demagogues. It had no definite meaning. James Madison himself could not have drawn a paper in which the sense of that Free Trade used as the battle-cry of the war was adequately explained. The

Sailors' Rights were also dim and far between. Certainly, Great Britain had been abusive and arrogant on the high seas. She had seized and searched American ships ; but it was with the definite purpose of finding an Irishman! She was not hunting for Brother Jonathan at all. She claimed then, as she had ever claimed since the Middle Ages, that the Irishman was hers. She did not propose that he should slip away to America and become a democrat. Therefore she arrested him in his flight. She did so under a code of international law which has long since been blown away. Tacitly the abuse ceased with the war of 1812, so far as American citizens were concerned, and to that extent the conflict had its value. But for the most part, the war was futile and flagrant, wicked and weak.

It was for these reasons that no great characters either of war or of peace were developed in our second contest with Great Britain. No warrior President arose to testify to the greatness of the conflict. Those who were great before the war remained so afterward, and those who subsequently became great did so, not because of the war of 1812, but without regard thereto. The score of years which succeeded the contest with the Mother Country was perhaps the feeblest period in American history. The citizen soldier had found in the crisis no cause of inspiration, no motive for those heroic activities which, when they are exhibited on an ample and fitting field, make men even as the gods.

Much of what has here been said respecting our last war with Great Britain may be repeated of the war with Mexico. The latter had in it many elements of popularity which were wanting in the former ; but it could not be said that on the whole the Mexican war was honorably undertaken or honorably closed. Certainly there is a difference between honor and glory. We got glory enough—and territory enough—from our war with Mexico. The setting of the battle-scene was picturesque in the last degree. The movement was so far away as to excite the imagination. Either a journey across the infinite plains of Texas, or a long voyage by sea was necessary to carry the American army to the enemy's coast. There lay the Rio Grande, the great international river, dividing the two warlike republics. Its appearance to the men of the North was like the Euphrates to the eyes of the Greeks of Xenophon. The land had the strangest of aspects. There were thickets of chaparral, beds of extinct rivers, smoking volcanoes in the horizon, a tropical sky in which huge vultures floated lazily, watching the camps below. Further on, the mountains rose; the pathway of the invaders lay over their crests. There the sublime Cordilleras lifted their summits to the line of perpetual snow.

The American army fought its way to the crest. It traversed the rocky pass of Cerro Gordo, defended by the best soldiers and best artillery of the nation. Then the invading forces, with the stars and stripes above them, swept on to the summit and looked down from those mountain heights upon the glorious valley and the far-off shining city of an ancient race. Then came other heroic fighting. Churubusco and Chapultepec still lay between the conquering army and the capital. But nothing could resist the onset. The city was won. The hero of Lundy's Lane, with fewer than six thousand men, rode triumphantly, in the glow of the summer morning, into the Grand Plaza, and the banner of the American Republic shot up to the glimmering spire over the halls of the Montezumas.

Every circumstance of the invasion—the country, the people, the landscape, the strangeness of the conditions; to say nothing of the glamour of foreign warfare and ever-repeated victory—conspired to give to this conflict with Mexico the form and substance, as well as the name, of glory. But when we reflect upon the vicious principles which underlay the conflict,

nd particularly when we look into the bottom of the
ap and see coiled therein the old adder of slavery—
or that, indeed, was the primary motive of extending
ou boundaries to the Rio Grande, the Colorado, and
the acific—we must, as many of our Whig fathers
did, rt back with horror at the injustice of such
gain such an end. True, the soldiers who fought
the batt s of that war knew not that they were hew-
ing the vay through the Mexican Republic, beat-
ing dow the national authority and exacting the
severest all treaties under the very knife and
bludgeon of ictory, only to extend the area of human
bondage; b the men who prepared and precipitated
the crisis kn full well the meaning and the motive
of the conflict. In so far as slavery was an ignomini-
ous institution; i so far as it cursed both the master
and the slave; in so far as it brought a blight and a
mildew on the fairest, the most fertile, and we may say
the most generous, part of the American Union—just
in that measure and degree was the Mexican war an
unholy aggression on a sister state, a great iniquity
done in the sight of earth and heaven.

The men of the war came home from their heroic
discipline in the land of the ancient Aztecs. They
brought with them victory and fame. They were
received with shouts, and were justly regarded as

the upholders of the national honor, the defenders of
the reputation of the American soldiery. Neverthe
less, the war with the Mexican Republic was not a
citizen soldier's war. In the first battles there were no
volunteers. The conflict lacked the essential elements
of truth and righteousness and conscience. It partook
too much of the nature of conquest and brutal triumph
over a fallen foe. It was a war between unequals
won by the stronger.   On the whole, it may be
doubted whether the reputation of the great United
States in the days to come, and at the solemn bar
of history, will not be dimmed rather than brightened
by the conquering invasion which our armies made
beyond the Rio Grande in the summer of '47.

Now it was that our American territories spread
out in one broad band from ocean to ocean.   The
wrong to Mexico, whatever it was, was done.   The
English-speaking race had moved forward its outposts
to Paso del Norte, to the Gulf of California, and to
those vast solitudes of the great Northwest

> "Where rolls the Oregon, and hears no sound
> Save his own dashings."

We had now attained the proportions of an empire.
More than three millions of square miles were ours.
Rivers and lakes and plains were ours.   Illimitable
prairies and the snow-crowned Rockies were ours.

Iron and coal, and silver and gold, were ours. Progress and power, multiplying states and a teeming people—resolute, vigorous ; heated with the fires of a thousand enterprises — were ours. Reputation at home and abroad was ours. The charm of the American Republic had diffused itself through all lands, from the foothills of Burmah to the upper fountains of the River Amazon. If we had only been just ; if we had only lived by the Declaration of Independence ; if we had only dared to say that "all men" MEANT all men, we might, indeed, have gone forward with unimpeded strides to an immortal destiny.

But sin was at the door. That ancient crime, old as the first victory of the human brute over his fellow—that primal, heaviest curse under which the civilized life of man has groaned even from the barbarous ages of antiquity — coiled around the root of the American tree, and its blossoms became poisonous, its fruit as the apples of Sodom, and its dews as the dews of the fabled Upas. No language can describe, no imagination conceive, the social, political, and moral condition into which this great country had sunk at the middle of our century. We had nearly all fallen under the dominion of the same fallacy, the same horrid delusion. The judgment of the American people was corrupted and its conscience depraved by the criminal disease of slavery.

Our children will have need to see the authentic testimony ere they will believe the story of African bondage in the United States. The appalling shadow lay not only on the South, but on the North. The great States of the Mississippi Valley had been in large measure populated by the poorer classes from the Border States beyond the Ohio. Our fathers here in the West were poor men, who had been squeezed out by the cruel discipline of slavery and driven to seek their fortunes in the unoccupied wilds of the Northwest Territory. Unfortunately, slavery had left its impress upon them. They believed in the righteousness of the system. They had heard "Cursed be Canaan" from the pulpit. They had imbibed the malevolent principles of the system from the fireside talk of their fathers and grandfathers in Kentucky and Virginia and the Carolinas. They had drawn the poison with their mothers' milk from the very fountain of life. We were all besotted together. We all agreed that slavery was good and righteous and necessary; that the abolitionist was the enemy of mankind, and that his adequate punishment could be effected only with the tools of the Inquisition.

It now seems to us amazing that such a horror

could have possessed one-half of the United States
and cast its baleful shadow over the other half even
to the clear waters of the Northern lakes. We need
to be reminded that within the quick memory of
men still young, children were born and bred for
the auction block; that hundreds and thousands
of them were sold by their own fathers to slave-
drivers, in comparison with whose heartless cruelties
the bloody passions of bull-dogs and hounds were as
the zephyrs of May to the roaring blasts of Decem-
ber; that mothers with new-born babes were set up
under the hammer of the auctioneer in the market-
place of almost every county town, and were
sold with as little compunction as cows and she-
mules; that maidens scarcely yellowed with African
blood were compelled to stand half-naked, surrounded with gaping crowds, drunken and hilarious with
the excitements of the sale-day, and be handled with
the vile hands of the traders, examining their teeth
and arms and open bosoms and limbs, to discover
the signs of vitality as the reason of higher bidding;
that the rattle of the chain was heard on every
highway leading from our Border States to the
sugar-plantations, the cotton-fields, and the rice-
swamps where the dusky creatures were delivered
over to the tender mercy of slave-drivers, with whip

and branding-iron and bludgeon, to be scourged and burned and beaten out of the image and semblance of human nature, down to the blackness of despair and the ignominy of unknown and unblest graves. The lesson will be good for us and our descendants to the tenth generation.

We may be sure that such a curse as the system of slavery proved to be in the United States a half a century ago can not remain forever without arousing the indignation and the hostility of many a brave heart strong enough and true enough to rise in rebellion and smite it with a fatal blow. In our day of degeneracy and national crime the deepest darkness preceded the dawn.

I have enlarged upon the condition of our nation and people in order to set in a strong light the one great antecedent and bottom cause of our Civil War. I have done so to the end that our minds may be refreshed as to the true elements of that tremendous conflict. We here arrive at a condition of precisely the kind to call from the very ground the most majestic and resolute citizen soldiery ever seen under the circle of the sun. Here was the grand reason and motive which inspired the men of '61 to leave the farm and the shop, the hamlet, the village, the city, to take their places with musket and sword under the starry banner given us by our fathers, and to offer their lives by the sanction of an immutable oath that the land should be made whole and clean from ocean to ocean, from the Southern Gulf to the pine woods of the Columbia. We all remember how, at the outbreak of our War for the Union, men beat about to find some other than the true cause for the dreadful storm which had burst upon us. The American mind was still, in large measure, under the dominion of fallacies. Even the greatest were not free from gross misconception and misjudgment of the conditions which were surging around us. The Republican party itself failed and refused to avow the true principle by which it was impelled. It even denied the necessity of its own existence by declaring its willingness to save and perpetuate a slave-holding Union. It is true, however, that the Under Man, who is always sooner or later the wisest man, perceived more clearly than our leaders and rulers the real enemy that must be slain. Ostensibly our great war was a war for the preservation of the Union. But what had endangered the Union? Who had made the attack upon our nationality? And why? For what reason had nearly one-third of the whole American people come to despise the Union which the fathers framed for

us a hundred years ago? Why did the Secessionists
wish to destroy the national authority and to scatter
its representatives? Why were the sacred memories and traditions of the Revolution forgotten and
despised in that hour of passion and mortal folly?
Simply because the Union had become an impediment
and menace to the institution of slavery. During the
greater part of the century the national authority
had been held as a shield over the head and bound
like a girdle around the loins of slavery. He who
looks attentively at the history of our country from
1821 to the outbreak of the Civil War can but
perceive that the whole force of the Nation, as
represented by the government at Washington, was
devoted to slavery as one might be devoted to
an idol. It seemed to be the one great end for
which the Union was created to foster, perpetuate,
extend and guard that atrocious system of servitude
which the misfortune of our early history and the
avarice and cruelty of after times had entailed upon
us. All the waters of great Neptune's ocean can not
wash the horrid stain from our escutcheon. The
record is indelible, and the American Union will to
the end of time and the final assize of nations be
obliged to face its ancient sin and shame.

At length, however, a new generation arose in

the North, and in parts of the South as well, whose life and thought were no longer poisoned and perverted by the system of slavery. More healthful breezes began to blow. A feeling of repugnance to human bondage and to the agencies by which it was perpetuated and extended began to work in the national conscience, and a murmur was heard around the horizon which he who would place his ear to the ground might hear afar as the premonition of a great storm.

The time has now arrived when we may speak without prejudice or passion of that tremendous political transformation which, beginning at the middle of the sixth decade, swelled higher and higher through the ensuing three years, broke in a long line of foam across the prairies of Illinois when the tall, gaunt Lincoln declared that a house divided against itself can not stand, and rushed with a purifying tempest through the nation in the fall of 1860. Never has history presented mankind at a better advantage than in the rising of the American people against the aggressions of slavery in the soul-stirring campaigns of 1856-58. It was the coming of an army with banners. The very thing itself, that marvelous insurrection of the American conscience, was the prophecy of our recovery and salvation.

Then it was that the inventive genius of the Under
Man put the five F's on his banner and bore it
everywhere through the countryside and the streets
of his village. And the five F's stood for Free
Speech, Free Press, Free Schools, Free Kansas and
Frémont. In that day men found something worthy
of debating and voting for. The very fundamental
principles and groundwork of our American institutions were on trial in the fiery ordeal into which we
swept. It looked like going into a furnace. But
down in the bottom of it the eye of patriotic faith
could see men walking in the midst of the flames,
and standing among them was the shining and
unscorched angel of Liberty.

Now in the retrospect there seems no wonder that
the apologists, defenders, champions, and dovotees
of slavery took a fatal alarm at the work done in
November of 1860. The election of Lincoln was to
them indeed the handwriting on the wall. As they
strained their angry eyes in the direction of the
Great Lakes they saw in the blue sky the flaming
trilogy of MENE TEKEL UPHARSIN. They rightly
apprehended that the Power on high had numbered
their kingdom and finished it. They saw clearly
enough that with them and their institution it was
then or never. They perceived that slavery was

about to be pent up; that a rim of iron and wrath was about to be bound around it, and that no future revolution of public opinion would ever break the barrier. They also knew that it is in the nature of sin and crime thus hampered, bound in and compressed to perish by asphyxia and atrophy. Therefore they must suddenly exert themselves in order to revive and perpetuate the system of human bondage. But the Government now stood in the way. The national authority was about to pass into the hands of one whose strange destiny had lifted him to the seat of power and responsibility. His fidelity was already known to the lovers of freedom, as it was, ere long, to be known to all the nations of the earth. It was clear that the Union could no longer be used in the interest of the upbuilding, maintenance, and extension of slavery. Rather was it certain that the whole power of the nation was now against the spirit and the domination, not to say the fact, of human servitude.

It thus happened that the American Union became the object of extreme hatred and dread to the slavery propagandists and fire-eaters of the South, while at the same time it became doubly dear, doubly sacred to the opponents of slavery, since to them it represented the means and ministry of deliverance and regeneration. Thus it came to pass that we had a war FOR the Union on the one side, and AGAINST the Union on the other. But at bottom it was a war between slavery and freedom. Two principles had risen like spirits from the earth. The one was the principle of free labor and emancipation; the other, the principle of bond labor and proscription. As the armies went forth to battle, these two spirits hovered ever above them in the smoke of the conflict, and the conflict could only cease when the bright spirit had caught the dark in mid-air and hurled him down from the concave to the abyss of death and perdition. It was the grapple of Michael with Beëlzebub, and the struggle could only end with the overthrow of the angel of wrath, or with the annihilation of the evil genius who opposed him.

Here then was an issue in our American society which all might see and understand. It was not a question involving abstractions and casuistry for the learned, but a question for the judgment and conscience of the common man. The farmer could apprehend it. The wood-cutters in their breathing spell between the fall of the tree and their attack on the trunk could discuss the crisis and denounce the enemy. The blacksmith might hammer this living issue into the blazing bar of iron on his anvil, and the maker of shoes could drive the heel-spikes through so plain a question of right and wrong, of truth and falsehood. It thus happened that when the volcano broke into eruption, when the whole sky was lighted up with the awful glare of war, the people at once made the cause their cause, and devoted their substance and their lives to the maintenance of the Union and the defense of native land.

Never before did a question arise which seemed so to shake, not only the American household, but the house itself. It was perceived that the conflict which had burst upon the country involved no less than the existence and salvation of American society. It was home or no home; government or no government; Union or no Union; country or no country; human liberty or no human liberty, not only for the present but for all time to come.

Such was the momentous occasion which evoked from the bosom of the American people that great army of citizen soldiers who arose and donned the blue in the spring and summer of 1861. It was necessary that the citizen soldier should come, and come quickly, to the rescue of the nation. How

impotent was the professional soldier in the presence
of that great emergency! How totally inadequate
was the American army to contend with so terrible
an enemy! A few thousand men, taught in the
tactics of theoretical war, and commanded by officers
whose ideas of actual warfare had been gathered in
Mexico, were scattered on distant frontiers watching
the dangerous antics of Indians. Many — perhaps
a majority — of the few who composed the ranks of
the regular army were men of the South, whose
sympathies, as the sequel showed, were with the
Secession cause and with the evil institution which
gave that cause its vehemence and vitality. Truly,
if the American Union had had to depend, in that
trying ordeal, upon the army which the nation possessed, then indeed would there have come a universal wreck and cataclysm in which all things would
have rushed down together. The Constitution of the
United States would have been blown to fragments,
and the watcher on the mountain tops, as he gazed
upon the throbbing of the earthquake, would have
seen the monument of Washington and the dome of
the Capitol nod and totter and crash down into a
hopeless and endless oblivion.

Certainly I do not disparage the noble band of
regulars who, called by the voice of the nation,

responded quickly and became a sort of nucleus
around which the living masses of the great citizen
soldiery were gathered. Much less would I disparage
those patriotic officers who, whether in the field or
in the ranks of private life, remembered the duty
which they owed to the nation, answered the nation's
call, drew their swords and hurried to the post of
danger. I do not forget that the genius of the war,
that the skill of generalship and command by which
the war was at last directed to a successful end, had
been nurtured in the great School on the banks of
the Hudson. We may not forget that the Silent
Man of Galena, and the grim captain who led the
Union host with flying banners from Atlanta to the
sea, and that most brilliant young American cavalry
officer who on his black horse came flying like the
very genius of battle to Winchester town, bringing
victory in the fire of his eye and the flash of his
sword, were all men from the barracks and drill-
halls of West Point. But on the other hand, we
must remember—ever remember—that the great host
who followed the flag and met the enemy and won
the battle was a citizen soldiery, gathered suddenly
from the ranks of the people. We must not forget
how the brave boys emerged from their quiet homes;
how they were watched by mothers and sisters and

sweethearts with tearful faces and throbbing hearts and spirits that seemed suddenly choked in their bosoms as the stripplings marched away down the road, over the hill, out of sight, they knew not whither, to the terrible experiences, hardships and perils of war. They were boys from the country-side, from the villages, the towns, the cities. They nearly all had homes and loved ones behind them. They were young. Perhaps a large majority of them had never cast a vote. Their faces were still smooth and their cheeks rosy with the fresh blood of youth. Some had known hard fare and toil and poverty, but many had been nursed in tenderness and ease and luxury. The hands were often blistered with the first use of the musket, and the feet were worn and sore with the trial march. All hopes, all aspirations were in the breasts of that splendid young soldiery. The refined sentiment and the poetic dream were in that army as well as the spirit of battle ; but the one prevailing passion was a patriotic devotion to the cause of the Union, and the one inspiration was the ambition to fight bravely and well the nation's battle, and to win and bring back with victory a flag unstained and unpolluted.

The spirit of our age has brought out discussion not a little about the real character and composition

of the Union army. Many things have been alleged
about the social, political and industrial sources from
which that great soldiery was derived. At the time
when the battle raged, and even in the years imme-
diately succeeding, no one thought to inquire with
nicety into the character and origin of the Man in
Blue. It was sufficient, when the emergency was on,
that he was a good fighter, that he kept his bayonet
towards the enemy, that he was sound in body and
spirit, and that he meant to bring home a flag with
all its stars restored. After the lapse of a quarter
of a century, however, when the day of payment
and recompense has come, many persons—particularly our distinguished paymasters—have taken the
habit of inquiring into the origin—the genesis, the
exodus, and even the Leviticus—of every man who
wore the Union blue and fought the Union battle.
The voice of caviling has been heard in places low
and places high. It has been said that, after all,
the great army was a mongrel assemblage of strange
elements marvelously mixed. The debates that have
dragged along for the past ten years bearing on the
pension legislation of the country have brought out
a vast deal of buncombe, and also a vast deal of
scurrility. We have been told that the bad man
was prevalent in the army ; that the scavenger and

pickpocket carried muskets and drew pay; that the
rogue was quartermaster, and the gambler lieuten-
ant-colonel. The effort has been made to stigmatize
the army as a whole because a draft was made to
contribute to the ranks—to drown the fragrance of
patriotism in the bad odors of the bounty. The old
soldiers of the Union army are ever and anon obliged
to listen with ill-concealed wrath to insinuations
against the motives and character of those by whose
side they fought the battle a quarter of a century
ago.

Doubtless there were bad men in the army. It
need not be denied that the rough, the rowdy and
the roustabout sometimes volunteered, and were
sometimes hired to go. It would be strange indeed
if an army of ten hundred thousand men should not
receive a considerable contribution from the worst
elements of society. Of a certainty, fighting is not
a saintly business, and saints are not always required
to do it. We may admit that many men went into
the army through impulse, from caprice, or with the
drift of the tide. Others went from selfish considera-
tions, hoping for some kind of a windfall of fortune,
and expecting to go unhurt of wounds and dangers.
Doubtless it was not heroic for a man to be drafted
against his will and be obliged to fight from the

compulsion of a bayonet behind his back. All this may be conceded without dishonor.

Judging from the other aspects of human society we should expect to find a certain percentage of badness in the Union army. No body of men numbering a hundred or a thousand, to say nothing of a hundred thousand or a million, has ever yet been free from the weaknesses and imperfections of the common lot. We may even select our assemblage from the very best fountains of society, and still the result is the same. If we enter the hall of the secret brotherhood we find the order to be composed of men — not angels. Appoint your committee of only ten, and the ancient error and passion of human nature at once appear. Every church has its schisms and quarrels, its heart-burnings and its scandals. The social club is rent by feuds, and must watch its officers. The society for the prevention of cruelty finds its secretary whipping his wife, and the Sunday-school treasurer has unexpected business in Canada.

But these are the institutions of peace and virtue. They are planted in society for the special promulgation and guardianship of the flowers and fruits of truth and hope and philanthropy. What then? Shall we suppose that an army, a thousand times as great in its aggregate energy and activities as any of the local institutions of mankind in times of peace, organized for the very purpose and mission of violence, armed with muskets and swords and dragging whole parks of death-vomiting artillery at its heels, will be free from some of the incidental traces of depravity? Shall we suppose the fighting man to be more sanctified than the man who plows or gathers pippins? Is it reasonable that they whose very business it is to expose their lives to every species of hardship and violence, including the violence of death; whose mission it is to wound and kill and dash down their fellow-men on the battle-field, will carefully observe the Ten Commandments and become the only community of saints in the world? Certainly not. The expectation of such a departure from the common foible and sin of life is irrational and absurd.

It is the truth of history that, apart from the common weaknesses of human character, no such other aggregate of men was ever seen on the earth as composed the Union army in the days of our trial and conflict. It was not composed of adventurers, but of nature's picked noblemen who offered themselves for the ordeal and the sacrifice. The average intellectual and moral force of our great citizen soldiery was the highest ever known among the battalions that have swept the fields of war and conquest. The best and strongest of the young men of the nation were in those magnificent ranks of blue. A great majority of them could no more have been hired to leave their hopes and homes and loves behind, to sunder the attachments, to scatter the ambitions and dreams of boyhood and youth, and to take up muskets for the destruction of their fellow-men, than they could have been hired to sack the school-house and burn the churches of their native villages. Ah, it was the *cause* that drew them forth from every field and hamlet and converted them suddenly into men of iron and destruction. They went into the army an unsullied host. Even in the pitch of battle and the license of the camp they kept their hearts void of offense towards man and God. And whoever to-day assails their characters, attempts to mar the glory of their work and record, or even casts an inuendo against the purity and nobility of their motives, is the one prodigious and infamous scandalmonger and slanderer of human history.

These things are true not only of the men who fought to defend and save the Union, but of those who fought to destroy it. We may not overlook

the great fact that the Confederate army also was
a citizen soldiery. The Boys in Gray left their
homes, cast their prospects away and gave themselves to what they supposed to be the cause of
their country. The Confederate army, like our
own, rose from the earth when the tocsin was
sounded, and went forth to battle with the same
motives and same heroic devotion as did the Boys
in Blue. It will not do to disparage that great
Southern army. It was composed of as brave men
as ever bared their breasts to the thunder-blast of
battle. I can not, even after a quarter of a century,
re-read the story of those tremendous conflicts—
of Malvern Hill, of Chantilly, of Antietam, of Fred-
ericksburg, of Gettysburg, of Shiloh, of Chickamauga,
of Mission Ridge, of the Wilderness—without hearing
again the roar of the awful struggle, without seeing
the earth converted in chaos and the heavens filled
with sulphurous smoke, without feeling again the
throb and rush and wild passion of the scene, without hot tears in the eye and fire in the heart, without
recognizing—I had almost said applauding—the terrible charges and wild yells of those Men in Gray
as they renewed the hopeless battle and swept over
hillcrest and chasm on their way to a heroic death
for the sake of their Sunny South. It were a shame

at this late day to fail to recognize the valor and
fidelity of that great host which rose at the call of
the Southern leaders and went to its fatal end in the
bloody ditches which marked the limits and finale
of the conflict.

While we thus praise our foe, while we commend
the heroism and devotion of the Southern army,
while we honor with this distant eulogium the
splendid battle which the Confederate soldiers fought,
we may not forget or omit to emphasize the essential badness of the Southern cause. It is here that
the whole difference lies between the work of the
Union soldier and that of the Confederate. It was
not that the one was braver than the other. It was
not that the one was more than the other inflamed
with patriotism ; though it is true that the patriotism
of the Northern soldier was of a larger significance
and truer measure than the merely local love of
country by which the man of the South was fired
to battle. The one fought for the whole nation, for
the Union as such, for the Government which our
fathers founded and transmitted to their descendants,
for the American name and fame in the widest sense ;
while the other fought for the State in which he was
born, or at most for that section of the United States
to which his own was bound by common ties.

It is therefore in the two causes for which the
combatants went to battle that we must seek the
real ground of divergence and the true reasons of
superiority. Nor is there any uncertainty as to this
matter of the relative place to be assigned to the
Union cause and that of the South. The question
has gone to the bar of history. The judgment of
mankind has been passed upon it, and a decision has
been rendered in that court from which there is no
appeal. The South has made a great mistake in
calling her cause the "Lost Cause;" as though any
cause could be lost that had in it the principle of
virtue and eternal truth! To say that a cause is
lost is to acknowledge that it is a bad cause, or else
to intimate that the world is a world of chance ; that
there is neither order in the earth below nor a
throne of righteousness in the heavens.   Doubtless
they who have coined and perpetuated this phrase
have thought to evoke the sympathy of mankind for
that great enterprise which the Southern leaders
projected and which carried them down in the tremendous wreck of 1865.   But the Lost Cause is not
a phrase with which to conjure.   That cause was
one of the worst for which men ever went to battle.
In almost every other attempted revolution which
has been undertaken in modern times the leaders

have challenged the good opinion of the world by
formulating some kind of document in which their
grievances and motives of conduct were set forth
to be read and pondered by all mankind. Thus did
our fathers in the summer of our Independence.
Were the rebels of '76, who rose against the Mother
Country, afraid or unable to tell the reasons of their
rebellion, to proclaim them on the housetops and to
cry them with endless vociferation and bonfire in
every village of the land? Nay, nay; they gloried
in it. They drew up a true bill with astounding
particulars and challenged not only the people but
the kings of every nation under the sun to read their
Declaration of Independence.

But what did the Southern leaders do? They
organized a rebellion. They fired the Southern
heart. They pulled down the Stars and Stripes and
trampled that sacred emblem in the dust. They
rent the Union asunder—tore their States out of the
Union's side as a tiger might tear out the vitals of
a victim. And for what? It is an astounding fact
in the history of our times that to this day the world
is waiting for that Southern Declaration of Independence. No man of them all, no number of men among
them, had the courage to undertake the preparation
of a document in which their so-called "cause"

should be set forth for the admiration of mankind.
The fact is that they had no cause but the cause
of Negro bondage. They had no reason for going to
war except the bad reason couched in the determination to hold the African race in slavery. It was the
reason of the rice-swamp and the cotton-field. It
was the reason of the auction-block. It was the
reason of avarice and that haughty spirit of domination which had been engendered by a century of
traffic in human life. It was a cause for which, with
sobered intelligence, the aged heroes of the exploded
Confederacy are compelled by the very logic of
events, by the unchangeable verdict of history, and
by the immutable judgment of mankind, to blush
and turn their faces to the wall. This is the one
great shame of their situation—that their cause was
infamous. To be sure it is not the business of any
patriot to taunt and harry the old Southern leaders
with their fatal and criminal mistake in making war
on the Union of our fathers. But the case is made
up; the verdict is rendered, and the documents,
under an unchangeable seal, have been handed over
to posterity. I hold in honor the Confederate soldiers
for their valor in the field, and I honor them still
more that they have rekindled the fires of ancient
devotion on the altars of the Southland; that even

in their old age their swords are ready to leap from
their scabbards at the slightest insult done to that
magnificent Union which they once fought to destroy.
I rejoice that by degrees they have recovered from
the wild insanity and fierce passions of that bloody
war. But I say that the fundamental reason and
principle which bore them into that war were as far
from the fundamental reason and principle which
moved the Union soldiers as night is from day, as
earth is from heaven.

> I say it ever and say it strong,
>   In that awful and bloody fight,
> The cause of the South was eternally wrong;
>   And the Union eternally right,

It was, then, the mission and destiny of our great
citizen soldier army to strike at and destroy the *cause*
on which the Southern Confederacy rested. It was
the portent and menace of such a cause in the United
States that had in the first place called forth the
Union soldiers; and its destruction was the one end
and aim for which they fought. I believe that more
and more, with the progress of the war, the true
concept of the issue was obtained by the combatants.
At the first the anger of the Union army flamed high
against the Confederates. The patriotic wrath of the
North, failing to apprehend precisely the nature of

the struggle, burned hot against the men who were the agents and representatives of the Southern cause. At the beginning the endeavor was rather to kill the Confederates as rebels and traitors, to sweep them from the face of the earth, than to annihilate the bad cause for which they had taken up arms against the Union. In the last year of the war, though the battles were as fierce as ever, though the determination of the Union soldiers to conquer or die became more fixed even than at the beginning of the conflict, the men who wore the blue came to look at the enemy in a different light. Intercourse sprang up along the lines; and it was easy to see, when the armistice was on, that the Men in Blue and the Men in Gray were after all but brethren estranged and belligerent. At the same time the Union soldier had come to see more clearly that it was a *principle* rather than a *man* that was to be destroyed. Doubtless the Southern mind also cleared as the contest drew near its end. Slavery was now hopelessly destroyed. That horrid nightmare had been broken forever; and only a few remained who desired that the incubus should again sit on the breast of the South. Many Southern leaders have in recent years declared that after the summer of '63, though the Confederates still fought well, even with a desperation of resistance for which it is hard to find a parallel in history, they nevertheless had lost the vehemence and fury of assault with which they began the war.

However these principles of action may be determined, it is certain that the true work of our Union soldiery was to purge this Nation of the curse of slavery, to make the Nation free, to institute by force a new era common to all the land, in which men might go everywhere with free speech as their right and free labor as their inheritance. This was enough. Free speech being granted, the time had come when slavery could no more exist in an enlightened nation than a moth can survive in the flames of a torch. The flag of the Republic had to be reinterpreted in its significance as well as lifted to its place again on every spire and temple within the borders of the Republic. American institutions had all to be explained in a new language by the agency of the sword. The jargon of political liberty had to give place to the reality. The Constitution of the United States had to be made consistent with the Declaration of Independence. For, know all men now and evermore that the Declaration of Independence, and not the Constitution of our country, is the true guide by which this new Nation so gloriously established by our fathers is to sail as with a chart and compass through the stormy seas.

From this point of view it is not difficult to perceive what should be the rational and patriotic attitude of the old soldiers of the Union towards their former foe. There is no reason why the men of the South should longer be held as enemies, unless in some particular instances they persist in hugging that old and miserable relic of barbarism which was blown from the cannon's mouth on the slopes of Gettysburgh and the banks of the Rappahannock. That the men of the South arose at the call of those who had been their trusted leaders; that, impelled by the forces of their birth and education, they took up arms; that, maddened by conditions which they could not understand, they rushed into a wicked war with the Union which made us one people,—were things natural, and perhaps inevitable, under the circumstances which had been inherited from an evil past. Perhaps not one man in a hundred of those who fought in the cause of the Confederacy sufficiently apprehended the nature of the thing he did to be held morally responsible by posterity. But after the fact, when the light of day has been turned in a flood upon the whole field of our national controversy, and when he who runs may read the unchangeable verdict of history with respect to the true nature of the conflict, whoever persists in hugging that ancient and delusive sin to his bossom is a criminal, and deserves the ostracism and hatred of mankind. The generation of men who were reared under the shadow of slavery, who were prejudiced and poisoned from their mother's breast with the malign influences of that pernicious institution, could not see the true conditions under which they lived, and can hardly be blamed for their blindness. It was only when the pall had been cut by the sword and when the light streamed through, illumining the land-scape and revealing to the senses and consciences of men the criminal condition of our political society, that responsibility came, bringing to every man the alterna-tive of choosing righteousness or sin. It is the part of the citizen soldiery still remaining in the land which their valor saved and redeemed from the blight of bondage to affiliate sincerely and loyally with all men, North and South, who are in love with free institutions and who uphold with heartiness and good will the doctrines of the Declaration of Independence.

We have now arrived at a point in the present review of our citizen soldier from which *his duties in peace*, as well as in war, may be deduced. One of the first of these was—and is—undoubtedly to cease to fight when the fight is done. The practice of war-fare quickly engenders a habit which is hard to break. Men are generally thrown into the army in their

youth, at that particular time of life when the mind
with all its intellections, its emotions, and passions,
passes rapidly from the mercurial freedom of boyhood
into the fixidness of permanent character.   The
young man who for three or four years about the
time of his majority is tossed into the indescribable
excitements of bivouac and battle can not with ease
regain his equilibrium and resume the tame pursuits
of peace.   This was the trial and hardship through
which the great majority of the Union soldiers passed
at the close of the Civil War.   To their everlasting
honor be it said that they quietly laid down their
arms and returned to their homes like men who were
coming again from a toilsome and dangerous journey
into a foreign land.

But another and still higher duty of the citizen
soldier in time of peace is to protect and defend by the
agencies of civil society the same principles for which
he fought when they were endangered by the violence of the enemy in the field.   It was not enough
that the men of the Union army beat down slavery
and secession by the violence of war and then
returned to their homes and country as though their
work were accomplished.   We all remember how the
principles involved in the great struggle with the
Southern Confederacy were put on trial before the

Government and people after the war had closed. The question of the Union, of the reconstruction of the Union, of the restoration of National authority, of the reëstablishment of the autonomy of all the States under the central Government of the Nation, was taken up by Congress; and for years together we journeyed on through seemingly endless discussion in the hope of finding the rational ground of settlement and peace. The question of the Black Man in particular, of his status before the law, of his rights as an American citizen, of everything that concerned him and his welfare, arose to trouble the mind and conscience of the American people; and to this day no clear and adequate concept has been obtained with respect to the African race, its present status and its future hope. These questions the citizen soldier inherited after the war, in common with the civilian; and the one, as much as the other, was bound to give heed and thought and effort to the issues thrust upon him, and to the solution of the difficulties which confronted the people. It would have been, and still will be, and is, the height of folly, the most illogical of all actions, for the citizen soldier, coming home victorious from his battle with slavery and with the Confederacy which was built upon it, to abandon or neglect any of the principles for which he

contended in the field. Now it is that the ballot-box
is substituted for the musket, the public press for the
ordnance train, the debating club for the commissary,
and the election for the blast of battle. Is not the
man who fought one way and votes another the most
prodigious fool in the world? Why should a soldier
expose his life to the hazard of war, face the enemy's
batteries, charge through the leaden hail of twenty
battle-fields, and come home with scars and diseases
bearing everlasting witness to the hardships through
which he has passed, only to turn about in his
relations and renounce in his civil action the very
principles for which he contended in the field? And
is not the citizen soldier more than any other man
in all the world under obligation to see the battle
through, to continue the contest until the victory is
absolute and the principles of truth, of justice, of
eternal righteousness written with an iron pen and
lead in the rock forever?

Let no soldier of that great Union army, therefore,
suppose for a moment that he is discharged. Never
until the comrade lifts the bugle in the gloaming of
the evening and for the last time sounds "taps" at
the brink of the soldier's grave can he be discharged
from his everlasting guardianship of those principles
of truth and right for which he exposed his life in

the war for the Union. The soldier knows how much the Union is worth. He knows what freedom cost. He knows at how great a sacrifice this Nation was redeemed and purged from its sin and shame. And he also knows that eternal vigilance in civil life, as well as in the life of warfare, is the price of that blessed freedom which his sword so gloriously won in the contest with the enemy.

Still another duty of the citizen soldier remains to be considered. He and the patriot civilian who was detained from the field, but who nevertheless had his heart, his soul, and his substance in the conflict — who with his sympathies upheld the flag and fought the battle at home while his brothers contended in the field—must be at one in all things, just as though they had been comrades in the camp. There has been a danger at this point in American society. It is a danger which has existed in all countries in similar conditions—the peril that a gap, a chasm, perchance an abyss, may open between the returned soldiers who have fought a successful war. and the citizens among whom they are distributed. For a while after the battle the soldier will of course be applauded for his heroic deeds ; but by and by the civil citizenship wearies somewhat of its applause. The shout is less loud and less prolonged than it was in the day of victory. Meanwhile the returning soldier, glad to recover his home sound in body and with victory on his crest, fraternizes with the civilian whom he left behind. At length, however, he finds his old comrade ; and they two begin to sit apart. Presently they look askance at the man who did not join them in battle. The question of honors and emoluments arises, and the soldier competes with the citizen, the citizen with the soldier. The latter expects the aid of his comrades, and the former says that the soldier after all fought not for the cause, but for the loaves and fishes. The breach thus started widens. It gapes ; and ere long the two classes, the soldiery and the citizenship, stand on opposite banks, all sympathy gone between them, watching each other's movements with distrust and jealousy.

Our own country has been happily spared the recurrence of this phenomenon in the civil and soldier life of the Nation. Never before did any soldiery subside so completely into its former relations and conditions as did our great Union army. But there have appeared at times symptoms of a class division between the old men of the war and the old men of civil life. They who opposed the war and had no sympathy with it have observed these manifestations of a possible break between the soldier and the citizen, and have rejoiced at the inauspicious sign. The Republic is to be congratulated that as yet no really dangerous rupture has anywhere occurred between the soldiers as a class and the civil population of which they constitute so honorable a part. It is the duty of the soldier to be on his guard against any and every condition and tendency which may threaten to place him in antagonism with his civilian neighbor.

The organization, now so widely extended and so powerful, of the old Men in Blue into the Grand Army of the Republic, was a movement altogether warranted by the circumstances, and natural to the situation. It was almost necessary that the surviving veterans of our war for the Union should in their after years seek the companionship and support which such a society affords. But even this great and honorable organization has its dangers. Some are dangers from within and others from without. There is a possibility of a soldier clannishness to the extent of making our outside citizenship distrustful of the order, composed though it is of the men who saved the Union. There is also a possibility that the veterans thus associated may doubt the fidelity of the civil citizenship with which they are surrounded. None of these things must be. Confidence, affection, mutual esteem and honor are the conditions which must continue to prevail between the veterans of the war for the Union and the patriotic people who have never borne arms. The citizen must continue to remember the soldier, to revive the tradition of his glorious work in the times of our National peril, to defer to all the righteous and well-founded claims which the soldier may have for the emoluments of office and the other benefits and distinctions conferred by society. Doubtless, the civilian is not expected to yield up his own ambitions, to deny his own capacities, to retire from sight and hide a diminished head in the presence of the Union veteran. Such a course would be ignoble, humiliating. All that is expected is that the citizen without a military record shall show a generous deference to the men who wore the blue.

On the other hand, it is the duty of the old citizen soldier to remember that his were not the only sacrifices and hardships that fell to the lot of the patriot in the trying crisis of the civil war. Too much honor can not be conceded to the men who remained behind and bore the burden of civil life while the Union army was doing its noble work in the field. It must be remembered that the men at home were also devoted patriots. Many of them were too old for the service.

Recollection is busy when these things are mentioned. Hundreds of aged men volunteered who had passed the epoch of strength, and were remanded to their homes by the mustering officers of the Government. It will not do to forget that.in the breasts of such the fires of battle were aglow as much as in the hearts of the young and strong who took their muskets, sprang into line and marched away. The passion for the service was so great that aged men went into barber-shops and had their white hair colored brown and their venerable beards cut away, that by such patriotic deception they might seem young again and be admitted to the ranks. Boys also struggled forward, and offered themselves at a time of life when nature could have by no means borne the weight of the service. Cripples were constrained to remain at home and fret about their yards with unsteady step. Those to whom nature had denied the gift of strength were left behind to sigh for the freedom of the march, the camp, the expedition, and for the wild excitements of battle. All these cheerfully gave themselves to such work as remained to be done at home. There were wives and mothers, and children in fatherless groups to be clothed and fed and warmed. There were a thousand sacrifices and hardships, means to be expended, farms to be mortgaged, homes to be encumbered or lost, resources to be consumed, and life itself to be worn away in patriotic devotion to such duties as the home service required of our patriotic people during the continuance of the war.

These things must by no means be forgotten. The soldiers must remember the steadfastness of the friends whom they left behind them. They must remember the loving messages which they had from loved ones on the field and in the hospital. They must recollect the boxes of provisions, the bundles of clothing, and the tokens of affection from father and mother at home, from sister and brother, from uncle and aunt, from the sweetheart who might presently be doomed to that indescribable widowhood into which ten thousand girls were plunged by the sudden eclipse of battle. If the Boys in Blue who took their muskets—with their lives—in their hands and put themselves between our American institutions and the enemy deserved, and still deserve, all things at the hands of the civil citizens of the United States, so in like manner that citizenship, patriotic and devoted to the soldier's cause both then and now, deserved, and still deserves, all things at the hands of the Union soldiers. The cause was a common cause, which some defended in the field and others maintained at home until what time the victory was won, the flag restored to its place, the curse of slavery extinguished, the secession enterprise buried in oblivion, and the Union reëstablished on the immutable foundation of righteousness. All who upheld and promoted that cause are entitled to mutual respect; and it is the duty of our citizen soldiery to concede the equal award of patriotism to their fellow-citizens in civil life.

Many things else crowd for utterance respecting the duties and work of the citizen soldier in these our times of peace. He is expected to instill into the minds of his children and his children's children the lessons of patriotism, of devotion, and of self-sacrifice. He is expected, in his life and character, to stand as the exemplar of all the nobler virtues by which the American people are redeemed and glorified in the eyes of the nations. He is expected to keep alive in his own breast the fires of his early love of liberty, and see to it that the sunset of his days is not clouded and obscured with pessimistic views of his country and his country's future. He is expected to exemplify in the last days of his earthly career the heroic dignity which belongs in all ages to the veteran soldier. He is expected, as the final ordeal of his life approaches, to face that enemy, whose shadowy sword no mortal life can escape, with the courage and valor which he exhibited in the days of his youth on the field of battle. He is expected to transmit to posterity an untarnished memory, hallowed by every ennobling circumstance which belongs to the life and work of the first men of the nineteenth century. He is expected to take his place in the shining ranks of the great and good whose deeds are commemorated and whose actions and names are made immortal in the ineffaceable records of human history.

Men and veterans of the Union army! The shadows lengthen. Your activity and strength are not so great as in the day when with fixed bayonets and flashing eyes you charged the vomiting batteries of the enemy. You are no longer young men. Already your ranks are thinned by the sword of the Destroyer. Many have gone to sleep in the valley, and many more totter in the last days of their earthly pilgrimage. The glow of the evening twilight is already around your camp. The sentries are already set for the night-watch which is soon to be called. The almond tree flourishes, and they that look out of the windows are darkened. Ere long the pitcher will be broken at the fountain and the wheel at the cistern cease to turn. Each succeeding year is transferring large numbers from your honored ranks to those other shadowy but shining ranks on high. Flesh and heart are failing, and the day is not so very far distant when for the last man of the Union host the shutters shall be closed and the mourners shall go about the streets.

As yet the day of the final extinction of that great army from the earth is for a while procrastinated. We may still meet and recount the battle. Many a song and jest and story may yet be sung or told by the rekindled camp fires of the veterans whose valiant arms won for us the fight in the battle which Freedom fought with the Dragon. Though the head is growing old, the heart of the soldier still glows with the fervor of perpetual youth. Though the annual roll-call is ever diminished, though gaps appear in the column to right and left, though well-remembered faces are seen no more on the anniversary day, though the green mounds, hallowed with flowers, bedewed with tears, and blessed with sacred memories, are ever multiplied, yet the remaining veterans close ranks, and with steady step march forward for the remaining battle of life. The blessings of earth and of Heaven be upon both the living and the dead! Sweet be the sunshine that lights, and soft the showers of summer rain that caress the graves of all our Union dead! May the whitening locks of our surviving comrades who still uphold the honor of the flag for which they contended so valorously in the day of battle be crowned with a crown surpassing the splendor of all kingly diadems, and the soul of every veteran of the Grand Army of the Republic be filled with the radiance of his country's smile, the warmth of the Nation's undying love, and the fullness of eternal peace!

www.ingramcontent.com/pod-product-compliance
Lightning Source LLC
Chambersburg PA
CBHW020332090426
42735CB00009B/1504